A Day in the Life: Desert Animals

Fennec Fox

Revised Edition

Anita Ganeri

Heinemann
LIBRARY
Chicago, Illinois

www.capstonepub.com
Visit our website to find out more information about Heinemann-Raintree books.

To order:
☎ Phone 800-747-4992
💻 Visit www.capstonepub.com to browse our catalog and order online.

Edited by Daniel Nunn, Rebecca Rissman, and Sian Smith
Designed by Richard Parker
Picture research by Elizabeth Alexander
Production by Victoria Fitzgerald
Originated by Capstone Global Library Ltd

Library of Congress Cataloging-in-Publication Data
Ganeri, Anita, 1961–
Fennec fox / Anita Ganeri.
p. cm. — (A day in the life. Desert animals)
Includes bibliographical references and index.
ISBN 9781484668238 (paperback)
1. Fennec—Juvenile literature. I. Title.
QL737.C22G36 2011
599.776—dc22   2010022819

Acknowledgments
We would like to thank the following for permission to reproduce photographs: Alamy: blickwinkel, 4, 23, 15, imageBROKER, 10, INTERFOTO, 17, 23, Juniors Bildarchiv GmbH, 5, 22; FLPA: David Hosking, 8, Mandal Ranjit, 14, 23, Yossi Eshbol, back cover, 20, 23; Getty Images: Floridapfe from S.Korea Kim in cherl, 9, 16, Frans Lemmens Images, cover; iStockphoto: Alan Hewitt, back cover, 18; Nature Picture Library: James Aldred, 21; Shutterstock: 6, Anke van Wyk, 23 (prey), BYUNGSUK KO, 13, ChWeiss, 12, hagit berkovich, 19, Martin Mecnarowski, 11, Nuno Miguel Duarte Rodrigues Lopes, 7, 23, Richard Williamson, 23 (insect)

We would like to thank Michael Bright for his assistance in the preparation of this book.

Contents

Some words are shown in bold, **like this**.
You can find them in the glossary on page 23.

A fennec fox is a **mammal**.

All mammals have some hair on their bodies and feed their babies milk.

4

Fennec foxes are the smallest foxes.

This adult fennec fox is about the same size as a pet cat.

Where Do Fennec Foxes Live?

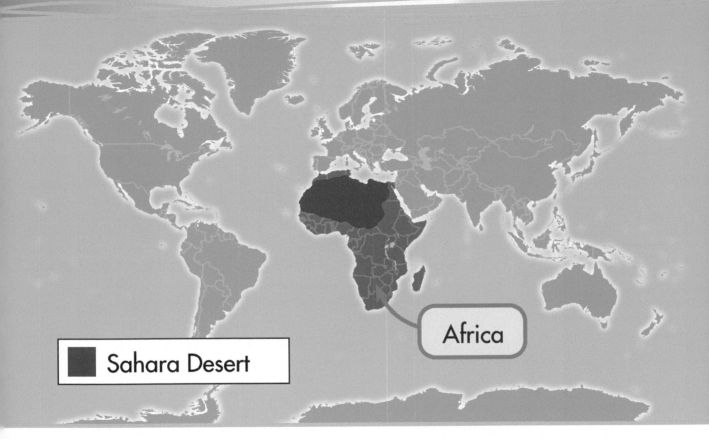

Africa

Sahara Desert

Most fennec foxes live in the Sahara **Desert** in North Africa.

Can you find this desert on the map?

sand dune

The desert is hot in the day and cold at night, with very little rain.

Fennec foxes live in **burrows** among the **sand dunes**.

What Do Fennec Foxes Look Like?

tail

Fennec foxes are small, with long, bushy tails.

They have thick, sand-colored fur.

Fennec foxes have big ears to help them hear and to keep cool.

Their feet are furry. This helps them walk across hot sand without getting burned.

What Do Fennec Foxes Do at Night?

burrow

At night, foxes come out of their **burrows** to hunt for food.

Their fur coats help to keep them warm.

A fox uses its big ears to find food in the dark.

It listens closely for the sound of its **prey** moving around.

What Do Fennec Foxes Eat?

grasshopper

Fennec foxes mostly hunt **desert insects**, such as grasshoppers and locusts.

They also eat mice, lizards, birds, and eggs.

The foxes do not need to drink water.

They get all the water they need from the food they eat.

hyena

A fox has to listen closely for nighttime hunters, such as hyenas.

If there is danger, a fox runs back to its **burrow**.

eagle owl

Eagle owls also hunt and eat fennec foxes.

Some people hunt fennec foxes for their meat and fur, or to keep them as pets.

Do Fennec Foxes Live in Groups?

Fennec foxes hunt on their own at night.

But the rest of the time, they live in family groups of up to 10 foxes.

sand dune

burrow

A family of foxes lives together in a **burrow** deep inside the **sand dunes**.

The foxes dig their burrows with their feet.

What Do Fennec Foxes Do During the Day?

During the day, it is very hot in the **desert**.

The foxes sleep in their **burrows**, where it is cooler.

If a fox goes outside, its sand-colored fur helps to hide it from **predators**.

Its huge ears give off heat to help it keep cool.

What Are Baby Fennec Foxes Called?

Baby fennec foxes are called **cubs**.

Their eyes open about 10 days after they are born.

The female stays in the **burrow** with the cubs.

The male guards the burrow from **predators** and brings food for the cubs.

Fennec Fox Body Map

ears

tail

fur

eye

mouth

feet

whiskers

Glossary

 **burrow** hole in the ground where a fennec fox lives

 **cub** young or baby fox

 **desert** very dry place that is rocky, stony, or sandy

 **insect** animal that has six legs, such as a grasshopper or an ant

 **mammal** animal that feeds its babies milk. All mammals have some hair or fur on their bodies.

 **predator** animal that hunts other animals for food

 **prey** animal that is eaten by other animals

 **sand dune** big pile of sand blown into a heap by the wind

Find Out More

Books

Haldane, Elizabeth. *Desert: Around the Clock with the Animals of the Desert* (24 Hours). New York: Dorling Kindersley, 2006.

Hodge, Deborah. *Desert Animals* (Who Lives Here?). Toronto: Kids Can Press, 2008.

MacAulay, Kelley, and Bobbie Kalman. *Desert Habitat* (Introducing Habitats). New York: Crabtree, 2008.

Websites

Learn more about fennec foxes at: **http://kids.nationalgeographic.com/kids/animals/creaturefeature/fennec-foxes**

Learn more facts about fennec foxes at: **http://nationalzoo.si.edu/Animals/SmallMammals/fact-fennecfox.cfm**

Index